What Would You Pack for an Adventure?

by Mrs. Anderson's class
with Tony Stead

capstone

Imagine you were asked to explore some of the most extreme landforms with your friends. Which ones would you choose? Our class had the opportunity to become landform experts. We will take you through the mountains, into caves, across a cold desert, to some islands, and even up a volcano! Don't worry, we'll be sure you are prepared to survive our adventure! Join us!

cave

island

cold desert

volcano

Mountains

by Angel, Bryce, Ian, Kali, and Mikayla,

What Is a Mountain?

What's tall, hard, and rocky? Mountains! Mountains are different from hills because they are much bigger. At the bottom, or base, of a mountain, it can be warm. But as you go up higher, it gets colder and the air gets thinner. At the top it could be freezing! Brrrr!

Where Are Mountains Found?

Mountains are found on all seven continents. Some of the coldest mountains are in Antarctica, and some of the hottest ones are the volcanic mountains in Hawaii. Mount Everest, between Tibet and Nepal, is the highest mountain. It is 29,029 feet tall.

But there is a mountain that's even taller if you measure it from its base, which is underwater. Mauna Kea in Hawaii is 13,796 feet above sea level. But from its base it's over 33,000 feet tall!

How Are Mountains Formed?

Huge pieces of rock called tectonic plates float inside the earth. Sometimes these plates crash into each other. When they move, their edges bump into each other and can get crushed like aluminum cans. When one plate moves over another one, it causes the ground to push up. This is how a mountain is formed.

Want to Explore a Mountain?

Exploring a mountain can be fun, but it's also dangerous. Here's what you'll need to survive. First, you'll need crampons. Crampons attach to the bottom of a trekker's boots. What's a trekker? You! If you are climbing a mountain, you are a trekker! Crampons have pointy spikes on them. When there's snow, they're good for going up and down mountains.

Other important things are food and water because you can DIE without them. Water will refresh you after climbing for a long time. Food will treat your hunger with care, so you won't be hungry after you climb up a steep and high mountain.

You may also need oxygen tanks to help you breathe if you plan to climb up really high. You should also bring a first-aid kit, bug spray, sunscreen, gloves, warm clothes, and an emergency phone.

Last of all, you'll need a backpack. A backpack will hold all the stuff you bring with you. Enjoy your hike!

Caves

by Aydin, Chloe, David, Hannah, and Madison

What Is a Cave?

A cave can be just a hole in the ground or in the side of a mountain. Caves are usually large enough for humans to go inside. Some caves are filled with water. Other caves are covered in moss or trees, or just made of rock. In places where it's very cold, caves can be made of ice and snow.

Where Are Caves Found?

Caves can be found all over the world. The largest cave ever found is in Vietnam in Southeast Asia. It is 5.5 miles long, and in some places it is over 650 feet wide and almost 500 feet tall! Scientists think it was formed 2 to 5 million years ago.

How Are Caves Formed?

It takes thousands of years for caves to form. A lot of caves are formed when chemicals in rain eat away at rock, especially limestone. Waves hitting cliffs can make sea caves. Volcanoes can also cause caves to form and so can landslides.

illustrated by Alayna

Want to Explore a Cave?

If you want to go on an exciting adventure, then a cave is the perfect place to go! Here are some things you would need to survive and stay comfortable at the same time. The first thing you need is clothing to keep you warm and dry. The clothing should be lightweight, which means it doesn't weigh very much. This will help you get around easier, but wear a layer underneath to stay warm.

You will need a helmet with a headlamp on it, so you can see. The helmet is also so you don't hit your head and get knocked out! Wear strong, sturdy boots for protection and socks to stay warm. Bring gloves and also knee pads and elbow pads to keep from scraping yourself.

Also bring along a bag with food, energy drinks, water, a first-aid kit, and extra batteries for the headlamp. That should be all you need to explore this wonderful landform. Have fun!

Cold Deserts

by Alayna, Brayson, Delaney, Jack, and Lucy

What Are Cold Deserts?

When you think of a desert, you may be thinking of a hot, dry, and sandy place. But did you know that there are also cold deserts? Cold deserts are dry, but they are not hot or sandy. Polar deserts are cold deserts that are covered with glaciers and mountains of ice.

Where Are Cold Deserts Found?

Polar deserts can be found in very cold climates like Antarctica, Greenland, and the North Pole. Cold deserts can even be found in places like China and Africa.

How Are Cold Deserts Formed?

Cold deserts were created when glaciers slid down hills or toward the ocean. The glaciers left snow and ice wherever they went. They are also cold and frozen because of their location in cold climates.

Want to Explore a Cold Desert?

If you want to explore a cold desert, you better bundle up! The good thing is you can walk for miles and not sweat one bit! If you go to a polar desert, you will need snow boots, a warm coat, and lots of layers of thick clothes. You'll also need a warm hat, warm gloves, and a face mask.

To visit a polar desert, you'll need snowshoes to strap onto your boots, ice picks, and something to start a fire if you need to keep warm or cook. Be sure to bundle up, and bring a camera to take pictures of this amazing landform.

Islands

by Abby, Brooke, Darius, Maddie, and Maggie

What Is an Island?

An island is land surrounded by water. Islands are not connected to a continent.

Where Are Islands Found?

Islands can be found in bodies of water off of every continent. They are located in all of the oceans. Islands can even be found in lakes and rivers.

Did you know that there are over 175,000 islands on Earth? Sometimes islands are in big groups, but they can also be alone. Finland has the most islands of any country. Greenland is the largest island in the world.

How Are Islands Formed?

There are several ways an island is formed. An oceanic island is made from a volcano. After the volcano erupts, the lava dries and forms the island. The Hawaiian Islands are examples of oceanic islands. Continental islands, on the other hand, were once connected to a continent and broke off. Greenland and Madagascar are examples of continental islands.

Did you know there is also something called an artificial island? They are man-made. There are artificial islands in Dubai that are shaped like palm trees. That would take awhile!

Want to Explore an Island?

The first thing you would need is a plane or boat to get you there! Unless you are a great swimmer! On the warm islands you can wear sandals, shorts, and T-shirts, but also remember your sunscreen and sunglasses. You may want to bring a swimsuit and snorkel to explore the ocean a bit. If you are going to an island that is famous for its warm, sunny weather, you may want to bring a camera and money to go fishing, diving, or dolphin- or whale-watching. You could also walk along the beach and hunt for shells. You can even explore volcanoes on some islands. You can read about what you need for that next.

Volcanoes

by Brandon, Brock, Brooklyn, Kyndra, and Quentin

What Is a Volcano?

Boom! A volcano erupts. A volcano is a hole in the earth's crust. Volcanoes erupt when gas and magma, or hot liquid rock, build up beneath Earth's surface. When a volcano erupts, gases, rocks, hot ash, and lava explode from its top.

Where Are Volcanoes Found?

The world has more than 1,500 volcanoes. Many are found in a region in the Pacific Ocean called the Ring of Fire. There is also a chain of ancient volcanoes that stretches all the way from Hawaii to Russia! You can also find volcanoes in places like Japan, Italy, Mexico, and South America.

How Are Volcanoes Formed?

Volcanoes are formed by tectonic plates, which are huge pieces of rock below the earth. Sometimes the plates will sink or float toward each other or move apart. When one tectonic plate sinks below another, it makes the rock so hot that it melts it. This molten rock slowly makes its way to the surface of the earth through cracks. When it reaches the surface, it is called lava. As lava builds up, a volcano is formed. Volcanoes can stay inactive, or not erupt, for many years.

Want to Explore a Volcano?

If you want to explore a volcano, make sure it's NOT an active one! Here's what you'll need to be safe:

- Sturdy shoes for climbing
- Eye protection
- A battery-powered radio to hear important messages or warning signals
- A flashlight with extra batteries in case it is dark
- A first-aid kit in case you get hurt
- A cell phone with GPS in case you get lost
- You'll also want to bring water just in case you get thirsty and emergency food because it's not like you're going to find any meatball subs up there. Be safe and have a fun trip!

first aid kit
Flashlight
Batteries
Emergency food
Sturdy Shoes
Meds
Breath Protection
Eye protection
Battery power Radio
Things you will need to explore a volcano!

We've explored mountains, caves, cold deserts, islands, and volcanoes. Which was your favorite? I'm glad we all survived and had a fun adventure! Use the map below to find some other amazing places to explore. What would you pack for that adventure?

Landforms Map